ROMANS

FACTS ● THINGS TO MAKE ● ACTIVITIES

NICOLA BAXTER

Franklin Watts

New York ● London ● Toronto ● Sydney

© Franklin Watts 1992

Franklin Watts, Inc.
95 Madison Avenue
New York, NY 10016

Library of Congress Cataloging-in-Publication Data

Baxter, Nicola.
    The Romans: facts, things to make, activities/Nicola Baxter.
        p. cm. – (Craft topics)
    Includes bibliographical references (p.   ) and index.
    Summary: Describes daily life in the Roman Empire and provides
instructions for related crafts projects.
    ISBN 0-531-14143-8
    1. Rome – Juvenile literature.   [1. Rome – Social life and customs.
2. Handicraft.]   I. Title.   II. Series.
DG77.B39 1992
937 – dc20   91-39798
                                                        CIP
                                                         AC

Editor: Hazel Poole
Designed by: Sally Boothroyd
Artwork by: Nigel Longden   93-723
Photography by: Chris Fairclough
Additional picture research by: Juliet Duff

The publishers would like to thank
Kirsty Witkowska and Andy Witkowski
for their participation with the
photographs in this book.

Printed in the United Kingdom

CONTENTS

THE STORY OF THE ROMANS

Nearly two thousand years ago, the Romans ruled a huge empire. Large parts of Europe, Africa and the Middle East were under Roman control. Some of the names that the Romans gave to the countries they conquered are still used today.

The Romans changed the lives of people in all parts of their empire. They took their own language and ideas to every country. They built roads and towns. They made people obey Roman laws and pay taxes, but usually they let the people they conquered choose their own religions.

Jesus was born in a part of the Roman Empire called Palestine. We use the date of his birth to describe when things happened. BC means "before Christ" and AD stands for *anno Domini.* That is "in the year of our Lord" in Latin, the language of the Romans. 100 AD is 100 years after the birth of Jesus. The Romans are often mentioned in the New Testament.

We know a lot about the Romans because they left behind books, pictures, buildings and other things that we can look at today. Some of what we know about the Romans has been discovered by archaeologists, who dig carefully at Roman sites to find traces from the time of the Romans.

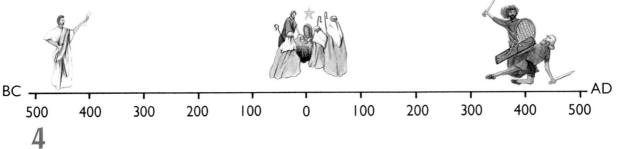

BC |——|— AD
500   400   300   200   100   0   100   200   300   400   500

WHERE DID THE ROMANS COME FROM?

The Romans took their name from the city of Rome, in Italy. We do not know very much about the early days of Rome, but the Romans themselves loved to tell stories about how things began. They said that a man called Romulus gave the city its name. When Romulus and his twin brother Remus were born, their uncle had them thrown into the Tiber River. The babies were rescued and raised by a female wolf. Later, Romulus built the first city of Rome by the Tiber River and became its first king.

▲ *This statue of Romulus, Remus and the wolf can be seen in Rome.*

THE REPUBLIC

It seems that the Romans were ruled by kings for over 250 years, but by 509 BC they decided that it was dangerous for one man to have all the power. A republic was formed. This meant that the rulers were chosen by the people themselves by voting at an election. This kind of government is called a democracy. In Roman times, women were not allowed to vote, and some people, called slaves, had no rights at all.

The most important jobs in the republic were done by the consuls and the senate. The two consuls led the country and the army. The senate was made up of senators. At first there were 300 senators, but later there were as many as 600. They gave advice to the consuls and had a lot of power themselves.

THE ROMAN EMPIRE

Soon the Romans began to conquer nearby lands. By 130 BC they ruled all of Italy and Greece, and most of Spain. Many Romans became very rich, but the lives of the poor people did not improve. People found it hard to agree on how to solve the problems this caused. In 27 BC, one man, called Octavianus, took control of all the Roman lands and people. He was given the name Augustus and became the first Roman emperor. This was the beginning of the Roman Empire.

Of course, the Roman Empire did not last forever. You can read about how it ended on page 28.

A ROMAN TOWN

In all the lands they conquered, the Romans built towns that they could feel at home in. Each town was built to a plan. The Romans liked things to be well organized and orderly. When they conquered Greek cities, they noticed that the streets were laid out in a crisscross pattern, called a grid. The Romans liked this pattern and used it in their own towns. Often there were two main streets that divided the town. Smaller streets led off these at right angles.

Every large town contained the buildings that you see on these pages. A Roman town in Africa could look very like a Roman town in Britain or Greece. Seeing what buildings a Roman town had in it tells us a lot about how the Romans lived.

The *thermae,* or bath houses, were not only places for washing but somewhere to meet friends and spend spare time. Large bath houses had restaurants, game rooms, snack bars and even libraries. Baths ranged from very hot, where people sat around as in a sauna, to very cold. Men and women either had separate bath houses or used the same one at different times.

The *amphitheater* was where shows were put on. Some of these seem cruel to us today. People could watch wild animals fighting each other or attacking people. There were also gladiator fights, where two men would fight each other until one of them was dead.

Many towns had walls around them with gates to let people and animals in. Just like today, there were often traffic jams! Some places tried to avoid this by only allowing carts into the town at night.

A *temple* was where the Romans went to worship their gods. The Romans believed in many different gods. When they took over a new land, they often took over the gods worshiped there as well. Some emperors were worshiped as gods after they died. Later, Christianity spread through the Roman Empire and became the official religion in AD 312.

The Romans were very good engineers. Their towns had sewers and piped water supplies. Sometimes water had to be brought from far away. An *aqueduct* was a kind of bridge that carried water across a valley.

The *forum* was like a town square. Important government buildings were built around it and market stalls were sometimes set up inside it. It was often the center of the city, where people met and did business.

Rich people lived in houses, but poorer people lived in blocks of "apartments," sometimes three or four stories high.

People could not be buried inside the town walls. *Tombs* were often seen along the roads leading into a town. The tombstones described who was buried there, just as they do today.

A ROMAN VILLA

A villa was the country home of a wealthy family. Villas were first designed to suit the warm weather of Italy. The hall, or *atrium,* in the middle was open to the sky. There was often a small pool in the center. The overhanging roof gave cool, shady places to sit in the open air, out of the hot sun. The marble floors were cool in hot weather, too.

When the Romans built villas in other, colder parts of their empire, they had to change them a little to suit the weather. A heating system under the floor kept the villas warm, and bigger windows let more sunshine inside.

The country villa of a very rich Roman might have been built in the middle of a huge estate. This one is surrounded by woods, fields and orchards. The villa also has a carefully planned garden with flower beds and pools. ▼

MAKE A ROMAN VILLA

You will need: two cereal boxes of the same size ● pencil ● tape ● scissors ● paper ● glue ● corrugated cardboard ● string ● large cardboard box ● trimming knife ● poster paints and paint-brushes ● blue clay.

Ask a grown-up to help you with this, as the knife blade will be sharp!

▲1. Seal the opened ends of the cereal boxes with tape. Draw a line all the way around the middle of each box. Carefully cut around the line on each box to make four pieces.

▲2. Turn the pieces upside down and glue them together to make a rectangle. This makes your villa walls. Covering the walls with plain paper will make them easier to paint later. Cut a piece of cardboard from the cardboard box, big enough for your villa to stand on.

▲3. On the smooth side of the corrugated cardboard, draw a line ¾ inch longer than the outside wall of your villa. Make a loop of string the same length as your line. Hold one end of the loop at the end of the line and put a pencil at the other end of the loop. With the pencil, make a mark above the line in the middle. Do the same on the other side. The place where the marks cross makes the top of a triangle. Join up the sides and cut out the triangle. Make three more triangles to fit the other walls. Make sure the corrugated lines run the same way on all of them.

▲4. Draw two lines on the back of one of your triangles. Cut along the top line. Run the points of your scissors along the bottom line so that it will fold easily. This makes one piece of roof. Do the same with the other triangles, making sure that the lines are in exactly the same place.

5. Use tape inside to join the four pieces of roof together. The roof will stand on top of the villa.

6. Now have fun painting and decorating your villa! Cut out doors and windows where you like. You can make a pool in the middle with a little strip of corrugated cardboard, filling it with blue clay to look like water.

EATING AND DRINKING

Just as rich people had bigger houses than poorer people, there were differences in the food they had to eat, too. This dinner party is being given by a very wealthy man. His guests lie on comfortable couches instead of sitting on chairs. They eat with their fingers.

The man giving the party had a lot of slaves to do all the work. They were like servants but they were owned by their master and had no rights. They could not leave if they did not like the work, nor could they do anything without their master's permission. Some slaves brought the food and drink. Others wiped the guests' fingers. Slaves also played music and danced to entertain the guests.

A rich man would try to impress his guests by serving very special food and wine. It might include ingredients from far away, such as spices from Asia. The Romans used lots of herbs and spices and ate animals that we do not think of as food, such as dormice! There was no sugar, so honey was used to make things sweet.

Food was prepared in the kitchen by slaves. To make sauces, spices and other ingredients would be pounded using a mortar and pestle. It was hard work! Food was cooked over open fires or barbecued over glowing charcoal. In summer, the kitchen was a very hot and uncomfortable place to be.

Poor people could not afford meat or fish or fine wine. They ate mainly bread or a kind of porridge made from wheat. Most of them did not have kitchens in their small homes. If they wanted hot food, they bought it from one of the many snack bars in the town.

Wine was stored in pointed pots called *amphorae*. Indoors they had to be propped against a wall. Outside they were sometimes buried up to their necks in the ground to keep the wine inside cool.

ROMAN ART

The Romans loved to fill their towns and homes with beautiful things. From different parts of the empire came precious stones, marble for carving, and gold and silver. There were many skilled craftsmen, sculptors, jewelers and painters. Luckily, many lovely pictures, statues and ornaments have been found buried in the ruins of Roman towns.

▲ *Part of Constantine's huge statue.*

Statues were very popular. Some were small enough to stand on a table. Some were life-size. Some people had *huge* statues of themselves made to show how important they were. This giant head was part of a statue of Emperor Constantine the Great. Turn to page 27 to find out how to make your own statue.

Today we hang pictures on our walls, but the Romans liked to paint pictures on the walls themselves. The artist would

begin to paint while the plaster on the walls was still wet. This made the colors very bright and helped them to last a long time—even until today! All kinds of scenes were painted. Sometimes they showed a garden or some columns that looked so real they made a room seem larger than it actually was.

Mosaics were also very popular. They were made up of tiny pieces of stone pressed into wet plaster to make a pattern or picture. The more complicated the pattern was, the smaller the pieces had to be. Up to one million pieces might be needed to make two square yards of mosaic! Some mosaics were useful as well as beautiful. This one was found at the doorway to a home. The words mean: Beware of the dog!

▶ *This "Beware of the dog" mosaic was found at the doorway of a Roman home in Pompeii.*

MAKE YOUR OWN MOSAIC

You will need: some eggshells ● poster paints ● a piece of stiff cardboard ● a pencil ● white glue.

▲1.   First wash your eggshells carefully in some soapy water. Try not to break them yet! Let them dry and then paint them with different colored poster paints.

2.   Decide what picture or pattern you would like to make, and draw it on the cardboard. You can copy a picture from this book or make up one of your own.

▲3.   Spread some glue over a little piece of the cardboard. Break off some pieces of shell of the color you want to use, and press them gently onto the glue. Like the Romans, you can decide how big your pieces need to be. But don't make them too small or it will take you a long time to finish your mosaic! Only put glue on a small part at a time so that the glue does not dry while you are choosing your pieces.

4.   You could hang your finished mosaic on the wall. Imagine how long it must have taken the Romans to cover a whole floor with mosaic!

SPORT AND SPECTACLES

Ordinary people couldn't afford to have mosaics on their floors, but they could go out to see a show. Often these were free, paid for by a wealthy man who wanted the people to support him. Many of these shows seem dangerous or cruel to us today, but the Romans enjoyed them very much.

▲ A charioteer races with four horses.

ANIMAL FIGHTS

Animals were brought from all over the empire. Lions, bears, zebras, elephants and giraffes were made to fight each other in the arena. There are even reports of the amphitheater being flooded so that crocodiles and hippopotamuses could be shown. Sometimes the animals were made to attack people. Not all Romans liked this kind of show.

SPORTS

Romans thought it was important to have a healthy body. Running, wrestling and javelin throwing were popular sports for men. At the bath houses men also used weights to help build their muscles.

CHARIOT RACING

This exciting sport usually took place at a special racetrack. A lightweight chariot was drawn by two or four horses. The drivers wore helmets and padded clothes, but even so they were often badly hurt, especially when the chariot turned the corner at the end of the track. There were four teams: the Reds, Blues, Greens and Whites. People supported one team and cheered on its drivers—just like supporting a football team today.

GLADIATOR FIGHTS

Gladiators were usually slaves from different parts of the empire. Often they had been captured in wars. They carried different weapons, but were carefully matched so that the fight lasted a long time. Usually the fight ended when one of the gladiators was killed, but sometimes a gladiator who had fought very bravely would be allowed to live.

▲ Many animals were killed at shows.

MAKE A VICTOR'S WREATH

The winner at the games or races was called the victor. He was often given a prize and a wreath of laurel leaves to show he was the winner. Why not make your own wreath?

You will need: some pipe cleaners
- paper or cardboard ● glue
- paints or felt-tip pens.

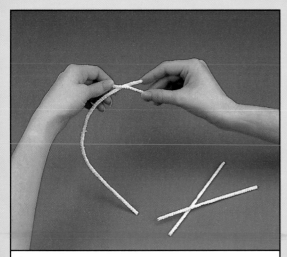

▲ **3.** Cut out each pair of leaves and put glue on the plain side. Fold the pairs in half around the pipe cleaner and press them firmly together to make one leaf. Do this all the way around the pipe cleaner. Some leaves should point upward and some downward. You can curl them around a pencil if you want them to look real.

▲ **1.** Twist some pipe cleaners together to make an open circle that fits around your head.

2. Trace the pattern below onto paper or thin cardboard. You will need to do this about 20 times. You could use green paper or color the leaves with paints or felt-tip pens.

ROMAN THEATER

Theater was something else that the Romans learned from the Greeks. At first they only put on Greek plays, but later Roman plays were written and special theaters were built. Like Greek theaters, they were D-shaped and larger ones could hold up to 30,000 people.

Only rich and powerful people had seats near the stage. Poorer people had seats farther away, high up at the back. The actors wore bright masks and costumes so that everyone could see who they were meant to be. The masks also funneled the actor's voice, just as a megaphone does, so that he could be heard throughout the theater.

▲ In this theater, awnings fixed to poles protect the spectators from rain and bright sunshine.

▶ This marble carving shows the larger-than-life faces of Roman actors' masks.

MAKE YOUR OWN MASK

Ask a grown-up to help you with this, as the knife blade will be sharp!

You will need: old newspapers ● an old plastic container ● water ● white glue ● a large cardboard box ● a pencil ● a trimming knife ● elastic ● poster paints ● yarn.

1. Tear the old newspapers into small pieces and soak them in water overnight in the plastic container.

2. Mash up the paper a bit more with your fingers. Then squeeze out as much water as possible and mix in some glue. Add enough so that the paper can be modeled into different shapes.

▲ 3. Cut out the corner of the cardboard box in a mask shape. Make it a bit bigger than your face so that it will show up from a distance.

4. Cut out two holes about the size of a penny for your eyes, and a slightly bigger hole for your mouth. Then draw on some features like eyebrows, nose and lips. Remember to make these as large as possible—they can be much bigger than the holes you have cut.

▲ 5. Use your paper mixture to build up features on the mask. When you have finished, leave it somewhere warm to dry.

6. Paint your mask in bright colors. To wear your mask, make two little holes at the sides and thread the elastic through.

YOUNG ROMANS

The head of a Roman family was the father. When a new baby was born, it was put on the floor in front of him. The father picked the baby up as a sign that it was now part of the family.

When the baby was named, a lucky charm was put around its neck. This was called a *bulla*. It was meant to keep the baby safe from harm.

TOYS

Some toys from Roman times have been found. Roman children had dolls and little models of people and animals to play with. They also played board games using dice. Outdoor games using balls and hoops were popular, too.

SCHOOL

Children whose parents were quite wealthy went to school when they were about six. They learned to read and write and studied the writing of famous Roman authors. Some boys went to another school when they were eleven. Here they learned more subjects, such as history, geography, astronomy, music and Greek. The Romans thought highly of Greek learning, so it was important to be able to read books by Greek writers.

GROWING UP

In Roman times, people often got married when they were very young. A girl might be 12 and a boy 14. A girl would offer her toys to the gods as a sign that she was no longer a child. Boys usually had a special ceremony when they were 14 to show that they were now grown up. They took off their childish clothes and *bulla* and put on adult clothes, including a *toga*.

Usually a boy or girl could not choose the person they were to marry. Their parents and relatives arranged it for them. A Roman bride wore a white dress and a red veil. The bridegroom carried the bride over the threshold of their new home. This was so that the bride did not stumble—that would have been thought very unlucky.

WRITING LATIN

Latin was the language of the Romans. They spoke it in all parts of their empire. But Latin did not die out when the Roman Empire ended. It became an important language of learning. The Bible was translated into Latin, and for hundreds of years important documents were always written in Latin.

You may already know some Latin words! Many English words come from Latin, with only small changes. Languages such as Italian and Spanish are even closer to Latin than English is. You have probably used some of the letters below without knowing that they are the first letters, or abbreviations, of Latin words. Do you know what they mean?

▲ Can you find any Roman names in this Latin carving?

P.S.	*post scriptum*
N.B.	*nota bene*
a.m.	*ante meridiem*
p.m.	*post meridiem*

The answers are on page 29.

In Roman times, important documents were written on scrolls. These were long rolls of a kind of paper, often 30 feet long. The paper, made from reeds, was called papyrus.

Papyrus was expensive, so children learning to write used writing tablets so that it didn't matter if they made a mistake. The tablets were made of wood with melted wax poured into the middle. When the wax was hard, children used a special pointed stick called a *stylus* to scratch letters on it. To use the tablet again, they used the flat end of the stick to smooth out the wax.

▲ This writing tablet could be closed up like a book.

MAKE A WRITING TABLET

You can use clay to make a writing tablet that works in the same way as a wax tablet.

You will need: a pencil and ruler ● a strong cardboard box ● a trimming knife ● glue ● some clay ● a rolling pin ● poster paints or felt-tip pens ● a modeling tool.

1. Draw three rectangles of the same size on the cardboard box and ask a grown-up to help cut them out carefully with the knife.

▲2. Put your ruler along the edge of one of the rectangles and draw a line. Do the same thing on the other sides. Cut along the lines with the knife so that you make a window. Do the same thing with *one* of the other rectangles.

3. Roll out the clay until it is about ¼ inch thick. Put one of the cardboard windows over the clay and use it as a guide to cut out a piece of clay the same size as the window.

▲4. Glue the pieces of cardboard together as in the picture, and put the clay rectangle in the middle. You can put a little bit of extra clay around the edges to make sure it doesn't fall out.

5. Decorate the edges of your writing tablet with paints or felt tips. Use the modeling tool as a *stylus*. You can write with the pointed end and smooth out your writing again with the flat end.

DRESS LIKE A ROMAN

Roman men and women wore all sorts of different clothes. It depended on where they came from, how rich they were, and what kind of work they did.

The kinds of clothes we most often think of the Romans as wearing are those you see below. They would be worn by fairly wealthy people, probably living in a city or town.

The woman is wearing a *stola* with a *palla* over it. A *stola* was quite a simple dress, often fastened with brooches at the shoulders. The *palla* was a large shawl that could be worn in different ways. Both of them might be made of beautiful colored fabrics.

The man is wearing a tunic with a *toga* over it. The *toga* was a very big half-circle of cloth that had to be carefully folded and arranged.

A STOLA AND PALLA

1. Fold one sheet in half lengthwise. Hold it up to your shoulders and ask a friend to mark where it reaches the floor. Cut across the sheet at that point.

2. Sew up the side of the sheet, but leave the top and bottom open.

You will need: two old single bed sheets ● scissors ● needle and thread ● string or cord ● scraps of colored cardboard and paper ● glue ● tape ● safety pins ● a friend to help you!

▲ 3. Make some brooches by using tape to attach safety pins to pieces of cardboard cut into shapes. Decorate them with colored paper shapes.

4. Use the brooches to pin together the top edge of your stola – but leave a space for your head!

5. Put on your stola. Tie two pieces of cord or string around you, and pull the stola up over them a bit.

6. The second bed sheet makes your palla. Drape it around yourself however you like, or look through this book for some ideas.

A TUNIC AND TOGA

1. Spread out the sheet on the floor. Find the middle of one of the long sides and make a small mark with a felt-tip pen. Cut a piece of string the same length as from the mark to the end of the sheet, but add a few more inches for making a knot.

▲ **2.** Tie one end of the string to a felt-tip pen, and ask a friend to hold the other end at the mark on the sheet. Very slowly and carefully, stretch out the string and let the felt-tip pen mark the sheet as you move around. You will draw a half circle. Cut along the line to make your toga.

3. Put on a large T-shirt that reaches at least to your knees. Tie a piece of string around your waist as a belt. Then ask a friend to help you put your toga on.

4. Togas were also worn in different ways, other than the pictures below illustrate. Remember, even the Romans found this difficult, so don't worry if you need to practice!

A Soldier's Life

To conquer new lands for the empire and to keep the peace there afterward, the Romans needed a large and skillful army. As the empire grew, the army became more and more important.

Controlling a huge number of soldiers is difficult. The Romans divided their army up into smaller groups of soldiers.

A century was a group of one hundred men, led by a centurion.

Each century was part of a cohort. Usually there were six centuries in a cohort.

Ten cohorts made up a legion. That is why soldiers were called legionaries.

In Roman times there were no trucks or airplanes to take soldiers to the farthest parts of the empire. They had to walk there carrying all their equipment. To make these journeys quicker and safer, the Roman army built thousands of miles of road all over the empire. These roads were so well made that some of them can still be seen today.

Most soldiers were infantry — they fought on foot. But there were also some horsemen, or cavalry, who were used for riding on ahead of the army to find the enemy.

Soldiers wore tunics and leather sandals. Over this they wore armor made of leather and metal. The armor had to be strong enough to protect them, but fairly light so that they could march long distances in it. Most soldiers carried spears and shields made of wood and leather. In colder parts of the empire, soldiers also wore woolen cloaks and leggings.

In training, soldiers practiced forming different fighting groups. One of these was called a *testudo*, or "tortoise shell," — perhaps you can see why. It was useful if the enemy were throwing rocks or spears down from the walls of a fortress.

When they were attacking a walled city, the Romans used a huge catapult, called an *onager*, to hurl huge rocks at the walls.

Legionaries came from all over the empire. Their lives were hard and they were often away from their families for years at a time.

There was always a danger that they would become fed up and rise up against their leaders. The emperors tried to keep them happy by paying them well and giving them a gift of money or land when they retired after 20 or 25 years of service.

Some soldiers built forts and walls as well as roads. Hadrian's Wall, which runs across the north of England, was about 73.5 miles long. It marked the most northerly border of the Roman Empire and made it easier to defend against Scottish tribes.

FAMOUS ROMANS

JULIUS CAESAR

Born about 104 BC, Julius Caesar was a great soldier. He helped to conquer new land for the Roman Empire, including most of what is now France. He returned to Italy in 49 BC and became the most powerful man in Rome. Some senators thought he was *too* powerful. They murdered him on March 15, 44 BC.

EMPEROR AUGUSTUS

Augustus' real name was Octavianus. He was the adopted son of Julius Caesar. After Caesar's death, Octavianus took power with two other men. One of these was Mark Antony. Later, these two fell out and Antony was defeated in battle. Octavianus ruled alone and was given a special title: Augustus. Augustus was a clever and fair ruler who took account of the people's needs, but kept a tight control on everything. He was such a good emperor that when he died in 14 AD, the people did not want to go back to a republic.

▼ *This statue of Augustus shows him as a powerful leader.*

▶ *This head of Claudius was found in a river in Suffolk, England.*

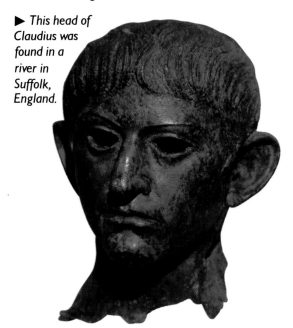

EMPEROR CLAUDIUS

Because he was often ill when he was young, Claudius led a quiet life, studying and writing history, until he was 51. Then he was made emperor because he was the only member of his family left. Although he was in some ways a strange choice, he ruled wisely until his death in 54 AD. During his reign, Britain became part of the empire.

EMPEROR CONSTANTINE

After 305 AD, the Roman Empire was split into an eastern empire and a western empire. Constantine the Great, as he was known, managed to unite the empire again for a while. He was the first emperor to become a Christian. He moved the capital of the empire from Rome to a new city in what is now Turkey. He called it Constantinople. Today we know it as Istanbul.

26

MAKE A ROMAN STATUE

Powerful Romans had statues of themselves set up in public places so that people would remember them. In Roman times, these statues were often painted in gold and bright colors, but the colors have since worn off and today we only see the color of the stone.

You will need: a 1-yard piece of plastic-covered wire ● some clay ● wallpaper paste ● cotton balls ● cotton fabric ● pencil ● scissors ● yarn or string ● poster paint.

▲ 1. To make a wire skeleton for your statue, first fold the piece of wire in half. Then bend and twist the wire to make a figure like the one in the picture.

2. Mix the wallpaper paste with water to make a fairly stiff paste. Tear or cut some of your fabric into strips, dip them in the glue, and then wind them around your wire skeleton. You can put some cotton balls around the wire to make the head and stomach fatter.

3. Before the paste dries, bend the statue's arms and head into the right positions for your statue.

4. Cut a strip of fabric as long as your statue, but not too wide. Make a hole in the middle, dip it in the paste, and slip it over the statue's head. Overlap the sides and tie a piece of yarn or string around your statue's waist.

5. Now spread out the rest of your fabric and draw a half-circle on it. The straight edge should be about three times as long as your statue. This is the statue's toga. Cut out the half-circle and dip it in the paste. Then drape the toga around your statue. Look at page 22 to see how to do this.

6. Make a mound of clay and push the legs of your statue into it. Leave it somewhere warm to dry until the paste has hardened. Then paint your statue.

THE END OF THE EMPIRE

Keeping order in the huge Roman Empire was always difficult. Many conquered people were unhappy under Roman rule and tried to rebel. The Roman army was kept busy acting as a police force throughout the empire. But problems came from *outside* the empire too. The Romans called people from beyond the empire barbarians. The barbarians were always attacking the borders of the empire, especially from the north.

By 300 AD, the Romans had divided the empire in an attempt to better control it. One emperor ruled the western empire from Rome, while another emperor ruled the eastern empire from Constantinople. But all the time barbarians were attacking the borders and invading further and further into the empire. The Romans could not defend themselves on all sides at once.

In 455 AD, Rome itself was seized by the barbarians, and just over 20 years later a German leader took over from the last western emperor. Strangely, this last emperor's name was a reminder of the very first days of Rome. It was Romulus Augustulus.

The eastern empire lasted much longer. It became known as the Byzantine Empire and kept many Roman customs and the Christian religion. But the eastern empire ended too, in 1453, when it was conquered by the Turks and became Muslim.

DID YOU KNOW?

SCRAPING, NOT SOAPING!

The Romans did not have soap. Instead, they covered their bodies with oil and then scraped the oil off with a special tool called a *strigilis*. Dirt and dead skin came off with the oil. Rich people had a slave to do the scraping for them!

THE ROMAN CALENDAR

Our calendar is based on the Roman one. Like us, they had 365 days in a year, a leap year every four years, and twelve months. Here are the names of the Roman months. Do they look familiar?

Januarius
Februarius
Martialis
Aprilis
Maius
Junius
Julius
Augustus
September
October
November
December

LATIN WORDS

post scriptum means "after writing" — a P.S. is something you add after you have finished writing a letter.

nota bene means "note well" — N.B. is used to point out something important.

ante meridiem (a.m.) means "before noon" — morning in other words! You can guess what *post meridiem* (p.m.) means.

ROMAN NUMERALS

Although the Romans were brilliant engineers, they were less good at math! This was because they used a system of numbers that were very awkward to do mathematical problems with. You can still sometimes see Roman numerals on clocks or sundials.

1	I
2	II
3	III
4	IV
5	V
6	VI
7	VII
8	VIII
9	IX
10	X
11	XI
12	XII

Can you see which two months were named after famous Roman leaders? Page 26 will give you a clue.

GLOSSARY

Abbreviation — A short way of saying or writing a word.

Amphitheater — A building in which shows were put on. It was usually built in a circle. Rows of seats rising around the space for the shows in the middle meant that everybody could see.

Amphorae — Pointed pottery jars for holding wine or oil.

Archaeologist — Someone who finds out about the past by looking at the buildings and objects that people have left behind.

Atrium — The hallway of a house, often open to the sky.

Barbarian — The Roman name for anyone who did not live in the Roman Empire.

Bulla — A lucky charm hung around the neck of a baby.

Cavalry — Soldiers who fought on horseback.

Centurion — Leader of a century.

Century — A group of 100 soldiers in the Roman army, led by a centurion.

Chariot — A cart with two wheels, pulled by horses.

Cohort — A group of about 600 soldiers in the Roman army.

Consul — A ruler in the time of the Roman republic. There were usually two consuls, who were in charge of the army and the laws.

Democracy — A country in which the people vote to decide who should be their leaders.

Emperor — The ruler of the Roman Empire.

Forum — The main square of a Roman town, where business was done.

Gladiator — A man (usually a slave) who was made to fight in a show to entertain people.

Infantry — Soldiers who fought on foot.

Legion — A group of nearly 6,000 soldiers, or legionaries, in the Roman army. A legion was made up of six cohorts.

Mortar and Pestle — A mortar is a strong bowl in which spices and other food can be crushed into a powder. The pestle is like a very heavy stick that pounds the food.

Mosaic — A picture or pattern made of many small pieces of stone set in plaster.

Palla — A large shawl worn by Roman women.

Papyrus — A kind of paper made from reeds pressed together.

Republic — A country where the people choose their own leaders.

Senator — A member of the senate, which was the body of men who gave advice to the consuls during the Roman republic.

Slave — A person who had no rights in Roman times. Slaves were owned by their masters but were sometimes given their freedom.

Stola — A long dress worn by Roman women.

Stylus — A pointed stick for writing on a wax tablet.

RESOURCES

BOOKS TO READ

Mediterranean Civilizations by Jean-Pierre Adams (Massachusetts: Silver, Burdett & Ginn, 1987)

Roman People by Hugh Bodey (Batsford; New York: David & Charles dist., 1981)

The Roman Empire and the Dark Ages by Giovanni Caselli (New York: Peter Bedrick Books, 1985)

Roman World by Mike Corbishley (New York: Warwick, 1986)

Roman Forts by Margaret Mulvihill (New York: Gloucester, 1990)

The Romans by Pamela Odijk (New Jersey: Silver Burdett, 1985)

Roman Legionary by Martin Windrow (New York: Franklin Watts, 1986)

PLACES TO VISIT

Check with local museums in your area to find out where you can see Roman artifacts on display.

Metropolitan Museum of Art
5th Avenue at 82nd Street
New York, NY 10028
(212) 535-7710

Items on display include marble carvings, sculptures, paintings, vessels, gold, silver, glass, and coins.

Bade Museum, Pacific School of Religion
1798 Scenic Avenue
Berkeley, CA 94709
(415) 848-0531

This excellent collection composed of pieces found on archaeological digs includes pottery, coins, lamps, burial crypts, and much more.

INDEX

Additional photographs: The Ancient Art and Architecture Collection 12(b), 20(both);
C.M. Dixon 5, 12(t), 14(b), 26(both); Michael Holford 14(t), 16; Zefa 28.